Longing
for the Endless Immensity

Reflection and Prayer for Living a Life That Matters

Chris Koellhoffer, IHM

Published by the Congregation of the Sisters,
Servants of the Immaculate Heart of Mary
Scranton, Pennsylvania

Longing
for the Endless Immensity
Reflection and Prayer for Living a Life That Matters

Within our hearts is a profound longing to live a life of significance, to make meaning out of our inner experience in ways that will enrich and influence our world. *Longing for the Endless Immensity* speaks to this collective desire and invites us to enter every moment of our lives as an arena for living contemplatively, for doing justice, for moving forward with intention. This book underscores the wisdom that no aspect of our everyday living is without impact on our evolving universe.

Each section begins and closes with breathprayer, offers a thought-provoking reflection, invites time for stillness and personal prayer, and suggests questions for journaling or group conversation and sharing. *Longing for the Endless Immensity* is recommended for parish groups, religious communities, adult faith formation, faith-based gatherings, peace and justice groups, and anyone hoping to leave a graced footprint on this earth by living a life that matters.

IHM Center
2300 Adams Avenue
Scranton, PA 18509
Phone: 570-346-5404
Fax: 570-346-5439
E-mail: communications@sistersofihm.org

This publication may be purchased at

Amazon: www.amazon.com

Barnes & Noble: www.barnesandnoble.com

CreateSpace: www.createspace.com/4850792

DEDICATION

With profound thanks to my Sisters of IHM
and to all who stake their lives on the dream
of a world blessed and sacred, whole and holy.

May it be so!

TABLE OF CONTENTS

Longing
for the Endless Immensity

Reflection and Prayer for Living a Life That Matters

Introduction

Imagine the transformation that could happen in our world if we lived with mindfulness, conscious of our place in the universe. If we claimed as our purpose for being on this planet what Thich Nhat Hanh describes as awakening from the illusion of our separateness. If we viewed every aspect of our lives, from the seemingly mundane to the extraordinary, as an arena for justice. If we prayed and reflected and labored as though everything we do lasts forever, because in God's time, it does.

What might such a shift look like? In such a space, we would more fully listen to and honor the deep longing of our own hearts and the hearts of others. We would hear both what is spoken and what is underneath the words. We would offer a tender embrace to all that is broken and fragile and vulnerable among us. We would dream both alone and together and grow rich with the wisdom such dreaming can teach us.

This book was born of just such imagining and longing.

For the past twenty years, I've penned a column for *Journey*, a thematic publication produced by the Sisters, Servants of the Immaculate Heart of Mary (Scranton). Since the invitation to write first came my way when I served as director of the IHM Peace and Justice office, the columns were to focus on some aspect of peacemaking and doing justice.

But how to do this? How wrap our desire for a more just, inclusive world in words that might inspire, intrigue, quicken one's soul, haunt one's memory? How shape a column that might challenge us to weep and rage, wonder and pray, and act with passion and graced intensity for the common good?

And then I stumbled on these words from Antoine de Saint Exupery:

If you want to build a ship,
don't drum up people to collect wood
and don't assign them tasks and work.
Rather, teach them to long
for the endless immensity of the sea.

That profound longing suffuses the prayer and reflection offered here and speaks of my hope for these pages:

May they invite us into reflective pauses and times of stillness;

May they challenge us to see every aspect of our lives as an arena for justice and a prayer for peace;

May they underscore both the global community's corporate ache as well as our intention to live lives of significance for our neighbors whom we may never meet;

May they beckon us to live contemplatively in communion with the universe, right here, right now.

A PROCESS OF READINESS
FOR SHIP BUILDING

These reflection pieces are designed so that they can be entered into during individual, personal prayer as well as in communal prayer and conversation. Be gentle with yourself and adapt the format to your own or your group's particular needs.

Breathprayer

From the moment we are born til the moment we die, we are breathing, thousands of times a day. Attentiveness to one's breath and how one breathes is part of many ancient traditions and includes yoga, tai chi, qigong, Buddhist and Christian ways of meditating.

In creation accounts, we read how God's Spirit hovered over chaos and breathed. The breath of God, the Spirit of God, was then and is now, generative, calling forth all varieties of new life.

At the beginning of each section of this book, you are invited into breathprayer, a simple tending to your own breath in union with the Spirit who breathes through you. Our hope is that this breathing with intention will also call forth new life for you and for our world. As you breathe in and out, welcoming air into your lungs and expelling it, you are invited to focus your breath on a few words that embody the theme of the reflection. Remain with this reverent breathing for at least several minutes to center yourself and open yourself to listen deeply to God at work within and around you.

For Reflection

These reflections originally appeared as a featured column in the IHM publication, *Journey*.

If you are using them for group process, invite each member of the group to sit with the reflection piece in advance of your gathering together, as this often makes the conversation more focused, attentive, and rich.

For Group Conversation and/or Journaling

If you are using these reflections on your own, you might want to use the conversation questions for writing and reflecting in your journal.

If you are using the reflections as part of a group process, it's helpful to have one member of the group facilitate this section. You might address the questions in the order in which they're listed, or you might invite the group to respond to the one question in the list that spoke to them most deeply. Emphasize the importance of each voice being heard and allow time for everyone in the group to respond before any one member moves into a second response.

Be sensitive to the group's comfort level, recognizing that sharing is a very individual response and that members of the group will enter into conversation as they are able. Some members may be comfortable sharing on every level while others may be more reserved. At the conclusion of the conversation section, thank the group and honor both what has been shared and what is still unsaid in the silence of everyone's hearts.

Breathprayer

The breathprayer is repeated at this part in the process. This offers an opportunity to sit with and reverence all that has evolved during the process, to prayerfully reflect on what has been shared, and to center oneself to move forward once the time concludes.

Closing Prayer

Whether praying individually or as a group, all are invited to pray aloud the closing prayer, which summarizes the theme of the reflection piece. Let this be a blessing for all who have come together in prayer.

Conclusion

If you want to build a ship,
don't drum up people to collect wood

and don't assign them tasks and work.
Rather, teach them to long
for the endless immensity of the sea.

The work of shipbuilding is labor intensive, full of challenges, adaptive, demanding careful attention and the giving over of one's time and energies. Ultimately, it's not only about the sleek lines and the finished hull. It's about who we become, alone and together, in the process of imagining the world we want to live in, then putting hands and heart into building the vessel that will take us there.

During these days of writing, I have prayed for and held sacred all of you who will enter these pages and work to create something new for the life of the world.

Blessings, and welcome aboard!

Chris Koellhoffer, IHM
April 2014

STAKING OUR LIVES
AGAINST DIS-ASTER

Path into the Holocaust Memorial
Boston, Massachusetts

Photo taken looking through the base level of the six glass towers which represent the six death camps. Six million numbers are etched into the glass walls, casting a shadow of tattoos on all who walk through.

When I visited Boston in 2012, I walked and prayed this beacon of reverent remembrance every day.

Breathprayer

Sit in a comfortable position in silence. As you
become aware of your breathing, pray this mantra or
one of your own choosing as you breathe in and out:
Breathing in: Nothing can separate
Breathing out: From the love of God.

For Reflection

What do you see when you look out your window?
What kind of world do you imagine waiting there for
you?

Some years ago, a natural disaster in Chicago
offered a frightening answer to that question. During
one summer, a severe heat wave gripped the city, with
deadly consequences. So intense and unrelenting were
the searing temperatures that hundreds of Chicagoans
died of heat-related complications. As the death toll
rose to over a thousand, news reports indicated that
many of the dead were the frail elderly, the very
young, and those whose failing health rendered them
especially vulnerable to the ravages of the heat wave.

But there were other people whose manner of death
was particularly disturbing, for some people actually
died of *fear*: they were so afraid of the world outside
their homes that they kept windows and doors closed,
and surrendered their lives to the overwhelming heat.
In a very real sense, it was fear, rather than heat, that
killed them.

Years later, I still mourn the worldview of those people. What they saw when they looked out their windows must have been so terrifying, so colored by despair, that they were driven to see death as a less frightening choice, perhaps the only choice.

In thinking of the consequences of such a worldview, I wonder what the children of this generation see when they look out their "windows." Do they gaze on a place where dreams are nurtured, life is celebrated, and they are cherished? Or are our children looking onto a landscape that is hostile, dangerous and disconnected in what Madeleine L'Engle calls the _real_ disaster? She defines "disaster" as, quite literally, "dis-aster—separation from the stars."[1] It's the equivalent of looking out a window and believing oneself and one's world without hope, devoid of light and promise.

Dis-aster is the worldview that the poet, Ina Hughes, had in mind when she prayed for all children

> *"who have no blanket to hug,*
> *who go to sleep hungry,*
> *who have no room to clean,*
> *whose monsters are real,*
> *who no longer bother to cry."[2]*

Dis-aster is revealed in statistics which shape the worldview of children in America:

One quarter of all children under five are poor.

One in every 45 children in the US is homeless each year.

A family of four living in extreme poverty lives on less than $32 a day

The number of children and teens killed by guns in one year would fill 134 classrooms of 20 students each

(Children's Defense Fund).

These statistics don't begin to reveal the price, in human terms, that poverty and violence exact from children. In the 1990s, just at the time Congress was considering shredding the safety net which protected the most vulnerable among us, Marian Wright Edelman noted that, for children, "poverty wears down their resilience and emotional reserves, saps their spirits and sense of self, crushes their hopes, devalues their potential and aspirations, and subjects them over time to physical, mental and emotional assault, injury and indignity...

Child poverty stalks its survivors down every avenue of their lives. It places them at greater risk of hunger, homelessness, sickness, physical or mental disability, violence, educational failure, teen parenthood, and family stress. It deprives them of many positive early childhood experiences, academic stimulation, and creative outlets...."[3]

Dis-aster is what Marian Wright Edelman rails against when she prays for children

"...who are sick from diseases we could have prevented, who are dying from guns we could have controlled, and who are killing from rage we could have averted by loving attention and positive alternatives;

...who are struggling to live to adulthood in the war zones of our cities, who plan their own funerals and fear each day will be their last;

...from whom we expect too little and from whom we expect too much; for those who have too little to live on and for those with so much they appreciate little; for children afflicted by want and children afflicted by affluence in a society that defines them by what they have rather than who they are—Thy loving gift."[4]

Obviously, the worldview we inherit as children has the potential to significantly shape the rest of our lives.

When I was a toddler, my family moved to the suburbs of New Jersey, to a home set on the top of a hill. My father, a transplanted native of urban Newark, embraced life in the countryside with exceptional gusto. Sometimes late at night after we had fallen asleep, he would shake us awake, wrap us in blankets and carry us out to the deck. There our sleep-filled eyes would slowly open to a midnight sky ablaze with stars. I grew up believing that my name was written in those stars, and a hundred astronomers could not have convinced me otherwise.

Since then, I've lived many places where pollution and artificial lighting have rendered the stars almost invisible. Still, I can't look at the night sky without believing in a future full of hope, for what I learned to see when I looked out the window as a child has colored my entire life.

In "Putting Children and Families First," the U.S. Bishops named the domestic crisis of our time as well as the commitment called from the community:

> *"Our nation is failing many of our children. Our world is a hostile and dangerous place for millions of children....We seek to call attention to this crisis and to fashion a response that builds on the values of our faith, the experience of our community, and the love and compassion of our people."[5]*

Can there be any lifework more critical than this: nurturing the dreams and shaping the worldview of children? Everyone who is a parent, guardian, teacher, mentor, every activist who struggles to effect social change, every crafter of public policy who protects vulnerable children and families, is a person co-creating what children see when they look out their window, a person refusing to let dis-aster happen.

Marian Wright Edelman further challenges us to insure that, when children look out the window, they see a future full of hope. She urges us to make that happen by covenanting

"to work together, mobilize, and vote to make it un-American for children to be the poorest group of citizens among us, or to be killed by guns, poverty, abuse, or neglect we have the power to prevent; to collaborate and work with each other and to seek common ground with any friend of children and to reach out to, try to transform—and oppose when necessary—any foe whose proposals and actions will make more children destitute, hungry, homeless, uneducated, uncared for, unsafe, or orphaned; to work together and mobilize to create a nation that welcomes and values every child, whose leaders and citizens place children first in word _and_ deed, and where 'the streets of the city shall be full of boys and girls playing in it.'"[6]

Together, let us work to create that city. In this City of God, the streets will offer each of us a life rich with connection and promise, a life without dis-aster, a life where every child can live Rilke's cry:

"Ah, not to be cut off,
not through the slightest partition
shut out from the law of the stars."[7]

For Group Conversation and/or Journaling

What do you see when you look out your "window"?

Have you experienced or witnessed the effects of poverty and violence on children? How did that affect you? What did it move you to do?

What is dis-aster—separation from the stars—for you?

Breathprayer

Sit in silence for several minutes at the close of this time.

As you become aware of your breathing, pray this mantra or one of your own choosing as you breathe in and out:

Breathing in: Nothing can separate

Breathing out: From the love of God.

Closing Prayer:

O Maker of the stars,
let us see your face.
Let us never lose sight of your presence
in us or the world around us.

Shine in the eyes of those we meet,
especially those for whom the stars
seem distant and impossibly far away.
May our hearts
and the hearts of our brothers and sisters
never know dis-aster.
Amen. Let it be so!

FEEDING THE LAKE: IT'S ABOUT TIME

Kayaker on Newton Lake
A place of peace and reflection on one of the many lakes in
Northeast Pennsylvania

Breathprayer

Sit in a comfortable position in silence. As you
become aware of your breathing, pray this mantra or
one of your own choosing as you breathe in and out:
Breathing in: I live this life
Breathing out: In God's time.

For Reflection

For several summers, I was able to spend one week
every August at a little cabin on Dam Pond, Maine.
I've yet to find anything that could beat sitting on the
dock on an afternoon brilliant with sun, drinking in
the unspoiled landscape. On one of those days, the
pond looked like mirrored glass. Not a single ripple,
not one visible movement, not even a gentle, lapping
current marred the surface of the water. It was
absolutely still and shimmering and ablaze with
reflected light.

And then it happened: a delicate dragonfly,
perched just a few seconds too long on the surface of
the pond, was gobbled up by a fast-moving trout. One
small splash, one momentary break in the stillness,
and that was it. End of story.

But that was not really "it." This micro-drama was
a moment situated in a larger context. It was, quite
literally, a ripple effect—and one with enduring
consequences. It was the acting out of Madeleine

L'Engle's insight that, "We all feed the lake. That is what is important. It is a corporate act."[8]

In a very physical sense, the fated dragonfly being devoured by the hungry fish certainly fed the lake, becoming a player in the great chain of life far beyond itself. But that moment also illuminated for me, now many years later, how we can presume to speak of "harvest" and "doing justice" in the same breath. "Harvest" seems almost a foreign concept in an area where we so seldom get to see immediate, tangible evidence that our efforts have effected meaningful social change. The definitions of harvest in the dictionary are not particularly helpful, either: as a noun, harvest is defined as "the outcome of any effort." And as a verb, harvest means "To get something as the result of an action or effort."

That does it, I thought, this is going to be the shortest peace and justice column ever! Harvest is simply not something we spend much time reflecting on in working for justice. Rather than pin our hopes on instant results, we try to put our energies and passion into being faithful to the struggle for the long haul. We may never get to see the harvest that our individual and collective efforts effect, but in faith we move forward, believing that what we do with God's grace does make a difference, and that what we become in the process of struggling together in itself transforms hearts and lives.

That pondside scenario of several summers ago underscores for me how Madeleine L'Engle's concept of feeding the lake and her reflection on time as both *chronos* and *kairos* speak to a harvest of justice. L'Engle looks at chronos as "time which changes things, makes them grow older, wears them out, disposes of them, chronologically, forever."[9] In this sense, once something is done, it's done. Over and gone. For example, a digital watch showing only the present moment is chronos. 1:45 is here, and then gone. That's it.

But in kairos, that's never "it." Kairos is time which is *not* measurable. In kairos, L'Engle notes, "we *are*, we are fully in isness, not negatively, but fully, wholly, positively. Kairos can sometimes enter, penetrate, break through chronos: the child at play, the painter at his easel...the saint at prayer, friends around the dinner table, the mother reaching out her arms for her newborn baby" —these are in kairos.[10] The hands on a pre-digital watch face showing the present moment in the context of a larger picture are reflective of kairos. Here, 1:45 is not simply 1:45 in isolation. It is connected and in relationship to 1:44 and to 1:46, to all that went before and to all that is yet to come. Time is seen as part of a continuum: yesterday, today, tomorrow, and beyond.

I've come to believe that when we speak of harvest in the same sentence as work for peace and justice, what we're really expressing is harvest that is in the kairos concept of time. In kairos, every act of love, every expression of our passion for a better world, has a life far beyond that moment. In kairos, we are in communion with all that has gone before and all that will come after. The consequences of acting in kairos have a ripple effect that is unending.

When Thich Nhat Hanh noted, "If you look deeply into the palm of your hand, you will see your parents and all delegations of your ancestors. All of them are alive in this moment. Each is present in your body. You are the continuation of each of these people,"[11] he was describing time as kairos.

In this sense of time, the human family is enriched by acts of profound generosity and sacrifice—mostly unknown and undocumented—that people through the ages have contributed to the struggle for a more just world. In this sense of time, both the great act of faith that is the planting of seeds and the satisfying act that is the reaping of a harvest are irrevocably joined in a continuum of grace.

This understanding of kairos underscores why the doing of justice on the grand scale has sometimes seemed to happen "overnight" and to appear simultaneously in many parts of the global community. Witness the Danish resistance to Nazi occupation; the chorus of hammering from hundreds of hands that resulted in the actual, visible fall of the Berlin Wall; the nonviolent witness of Gandhi and Martin Luther King, Jr.; the struggle for civil rights in the United States and the struggle against apartheid in

South Africa; the mass of students in Tiananmen
Square bearing signs that read, "Although you trod a
thousand resisters underfoot, I shall be the one-
thousand-and-first,"[12] and the unforgettable image of a
small, slender student standing alone in the face of an
approaching tank; the courageous strike of Polish
workers in the Solidarity movement; the groundswell
of support for workers' rights and against sweatshops
among high school and college students and young
activists around the world. All of this comes from the
flow of good works that is part of feeding the lake over
time and distance. And these are just a few of the acts
that we know of.

What is not publicized, affirmed, or even
acknowledged in chronos still has importance in
kairos because it is seen as part of the corporate act
that continues to feed the lake. Sheila Cassidy holds to
her belief that all our efforts for justice ultimately bring
forth a harvest when she observes,

"I believe,
no pain is lost.
No tear unmarked,
no cry of anguish
dies unheard,
lost in the hail of gunfire
or blanked out by the padded cell.

...The blood
shed in El Salvador
will irrigate the heart

of some financier
a million miles away."[13]

If we truly believe this, then our faithfulness to the struggle for justice becomes critical, for who can measure the ripple effect of one committed person, who, day in and day out, passionately, faithfully creates a loving heart and a loving world? We measure not the success or the dramatic results, but the continual giving ourselves over with love to the great corporate act of feeding the lake. It is all we can do, and it is everything.

Thomas Merton, in a letter to a young activist, observed, "Do not depend on the hope of results. When you are doing the sort of work you have taken on...you may have to face the fact that your work will be apparently worthless and achieve no result at all...As you get used to this idea, you start more and more to concentrate not on the results, but on the value, the rightness, the truth of the work itself...gradually you struggle less and less for an idea and more and more for specific people. The range tends to narrow down, but it gets much more real. In the end, it is the reality of personal relationships that saves everything."[14]

This is why St. Therese, the young Carmelite nun who never left her convent, could be considered a patroness of missionaries, could be lifted up as a model of outreach and impact on our world. She was living in kairos, and she fed the lake. This is why prisoners of conscience can keep hope alive in spite of brutal confinement and seeming abandonment. They are feeding the lake. This is why people whose lives are given over to long days and nights of caring for a loved one or laboring to support a family can know their compassion makes a difference. They are feeding the lake.

Is the struggle worth it? Yes, because in this feeding, no act of love is ever lost or wasted. In kairos, social sin never has the last word. Present realities, no matter how hopeless they appear, are not ultimate, and our struggle to transform them contributes to the great corporate act of feeding the lake.

In kairos, all that we do with love, however hidden and unacknowledged it is, enriches our world. Parenting a child into a loving, thoughtful person feeds the lake. Bringing gospel values into our workplace feeds the lake. Advocating for refugees detained in prison feeds the lake. Nurturing healthy relationships feeds the lake. Demonstrating for workers' rights feeds the lake. Mentoring a student feeds the lake. Companioning a lonely friend or neighbor feeds the lake. In kairos, we understand with Joanna Macy that, "Our lives extend beyond our skins, in radical interdependence with the rest of the world."[15]

This sense of kairos is illustrated in a most moving way when, each year, my IHM community gathers and remembers those Sisters who have died within the past year. Lifting up the collective witness of these lives is a powerful experience. In our beautiful sung litany of names of the holy ones, we know ourselves in communion with something far greater than our own efforts. We hear this roll call of risen life as a testament to those whose lives, individually and corporately, continue to feed the lake.

So the next time you're near water, give thanks to the God who creates oceans, rivers, lakes, pools, ponds, puddles for your delight, your renewal, your contemplation, your inspiration. Reach out to the water, splash, let the grace of the moment wash over you. Reflect how your life is in communion with all the holy ones who, at that very moment, are going about feeding the lake. Remember that here, in this lake, no act of love is ever lost, forgotten, or wasted. Remember that here, in this lake, it's about time.

For Group Conversation and/or Journaling

How do you "feed the lake" in your daily living?

Perhaps the notion of time as both *chronos* and *kairos* is new to you. Does this distinction excite you? confuse you? disturb you? console you? Why?

In the understanding of kairos time, no act of love is ever lost, forgotten, or wasted. Reflect on an experience in your life when you felt that your efforts were fruitless or your time was wasted. How might you view that experience in a new light from the perspective of kairos?

How might a sense of kairos influence your work for justice and peace in the future?

Breathprayer

Sit in silence for several minutes at the close of this time.

As you become aware of your breathing, pray this mantra or one of your own choosing as you breathe in and out:

Breathing in: I live this life

Breathing out: In God's time.

Closing prayer:

God beyond time,
sometimes we are held captive
by our need for results,
favorable outcomes,
immediate gratification.
Free us from judging success
solely by what can be quantified and measured.
Imbue us with your divine perspective:
that in the Reign of God,
no act of love
is ever lost, forgotten, or wasted.
Amen. Let it be so!

SENDING THE GREAT BLUE HERON

Great Blue Heron
This majestic bird, perched on a dock in Point Pleasant Beach, is a faithful visitor sighted and photographed by my sister, Teri, from her home in New Jersey

Breathprayer

Sit in a comfortable position in silence. As you become aware of your breathing, pray this mantra or one of your own choosing as you breathe in and out:

Breathing in: God sends.

Breathing out: We are sent.

For Reflection

Not quite ten years ago, my sister, Teri, and her family experienced a devastating loss: one Labor Day weekend, in the middle of the night, their entire home burned to the ground. Though there were a few items that could be salvaged, most of what her family had spent their lives cherishing was gone in an instant. Photos of the three boys from infancy to near adulthood. Videos of family vacations. Financial and personal documents. Artifacts of sentimental value.

This loss of home was multi-layered: yes, they had all escaped with their lives. Yes, they were all uninjured. But what about all the intangibles that had forever been altered in this loss of home: their notion of security and safety; their ability to protect their children; their feeling of belonging; their sense of sacred space?

Frederic Brussat notes that, "Our homes often demonstrate what the mystics know: that life consists of connections—with nature, our past, and other people."[16] And perhaps that's why, for my sister's family, the most unsettling loss was that of connection: to home, to neighborhood, to the familiar.

This loss of connection was underscored in the first year after the fire when the family moved in and out of temporary housing—at times with relatives, at times in a rental house, and at times in our late parents' former home in Point Pleasant Beach, New Jersey.

Soon after she arrived to stay at the shore, Teri got up one morning, opened the blinds, and there, knee deep in the water and standing absolutely still, was a Great Blue Heron. A magnificent and rare sight at any time, but for my sister, an immediate sense of home.

Before the fire, she had often walked by a lake near her home where a stately Great Blue Heron made a frequent appearance, so in her now uprooted state, she read the sighting of this bird as a sign: all would be well, she and her family would once again flourish and feel protected, and there would be a homecoming in her future. For as long as she remained at my parents' home, she and the Great Blue Heron followed their morning ritual as she opened the blinds: she breathed gratitude, and he breathed comfort and reassurance.

In reflecting on our sense of home and its connection to social justice, I find myself "sending" Great Blue Herons to many corners of our world. This past year has found us struggling with the impermanence of our place in the universe, as natural disasters in the shape of floods, tsunamis, earthquakes, fires, mudslides and hurricanes have wreaked havoc on the stability of countless lives.

In the US in August 2005, Hurricane Katrina and the Gulf Coast tragedy clearly underscored divisions along economic, class, and racial lines. Certainly, the great divide in the sense of "home" in New Orleans was glaringly apparent as those with means—

transportation, money, places to stay—fled the city as hurricanes approached, while those without—21,787 poor households had no cars—faced the terrifying prospect of remaining in the path of destruction.

In my prayer these days, I am sending a Great Blue Heron to all who have endured such trauma and abandonment by the forces of nature, by the state and national government, by the racial divide that leaves the poor in the most vulnerable parts of the city.

I am sending a Great Blue Heron to the people of Darfur, who have endured the longest continuous war on the African continent, a war that has left a death toll of 180,000 or higher, and more than 2.4 million people homeless. Compounding the loss of home is the insecurity of the region, making it unsafe for both civilians and humanitarian aid operations to remain.

I am sending a Great Blue Heron to every one of the over 45 million refugees and displaced persons in our world, 80% of whom are women and children. They risk serious human rights abuses because of who they are or what they believe; they cannot or will not return home because their government cannot or will not protect them.

I am sending a Great Blue Heron to the thousands of committed citizens who accompany or companion all whose sense of home has been stolen from them. As Jesuit Refugee Services USA notes, "Our accompaniment affirms that God is present in human history, even in its most tragic episodes."[17]

I am sending a Great Blue Heron in the list of suggestions that accompanies this column. May these suggestions for spiritual reflection and action deepen or enlarge our global sense of home. May our commitment to live lives of compassion and justice send the Great Blue Heron to wounded humanity and bring to fullness God's dream of a world where all are at home.

Suggestions for Deepening a Just Sense of Home

- Create prayers of thanksgiving for the different rooms of your house. When you bless the food that you eat, remember to also thank the room where it was prepared and the place where you are eating.
- Set up a home shrine consisting of objects, writings, or pictures which have spiritual meaning for you. Make it a place for reading, prayer, and contemplation.
- Hold a ritual to honor a special place in your life. Examples: the place where you have been most creative; the place where you began, or ended, a significant relationship; the place where you discovered something new about yourself; the place where you brought life out of death.

- Share a story about a particular place that comforted you or transformed your perspective about yourself.

(The above suggestions are taken from *Spiritual Literacy*, edited by Frederic and Mary Ann Brussat)[18]

- Bring into your home the beauty of other homes: music, art, poetry, and food from cultures or corners of the world other than your own.
- Contribute financial assistance or your time and energy to relief efforts on behalf of those who have lost their homes through natural disasters, war, or regional conflict.
- Take action to advocate for or change policy on behalf of immigrants, refugees, or those who are homeless.

Some good sources:

- Amnesty International (www.amnesty.org)
- Justice for Immigrants (www.justiceforimmigrants.org)
- Jesuit Refugee Service (www.jrs.net)
- NETWORK (www.networklobby.org)
- National Coalition for the Homeless (www.nationalhomeless.org)
- Habitat for Humanity (www.habitat.org)

For Group Conversation and/or Journaling

Reflect on a personal experience or news story of a natural disaster, an eviction, an accident, an act of violence, or anything that threatened a sense of security, safety, and belonging.

What was your response to such an experience?

What learnings might have come your way during or afterwards?

If Great Blue Herons were sent to you or others during this time, what were they?

Where in our world might you most want to send a Great Blue Heron today? Share the reasons for your choice.

Breathprayer

Sit in silence for several minutes at the close of this time.

As you become aware of your breathing, pray this mantra or one of your own choosing.

Breathing in: God sends.

Breathing out: We are sent.

Closing Prayer:

Sending God,
you are all we have, all we need.
You live and move and breathe among us.
Stand with us when our sense of home is shaken or
destroyed,
when the lives of our neighbors
and their sense of security and safety is threatened.

As we are comforted by your promise and your
presence,
may we be present to the most fragile and
vulnerable among us.
Amen. Let it be so!

TRACING OUR JOURNEYS

Yellow Hibiscus
An up-close look into the face of a flower, revealing patterns of growth and change

Breathprayer

Sit in a comfortable position in silence. As you become aware of your breathing, pray this mantra or one of your own choosing as you breathe in and out:

Breathing in: God embraces me.

Breathing out: I welcome the world.

For Reflection

Lately I've been reflecting a lot on stretch marks. Not the literal, physical kind, that scarring of the skin caused by pregnancy or rapid adolescent growth. Instead, I'm contemplating stretch marks that reveal the way in which a person's spirit or worldview has expanded enormously, sometimes explosively. Stretch marks that are the direct result of taking a risk, of opening up to a new experience, of struggling to grow emotionally or spiritually, of reaching out in attitudes of peacemaking or actions for justice. Like their physical counterparts, these stretch marks of the spirit may diminish over time, but they will never disappear completely. They're the map of where we've been and what we've opened ourselves to; they hint at future directions and possibilities; they mark us for life.

In one of the entries in *A Maryknoll Book of Inspiration*,[19] Wendy Wright describes healing from a Caesarean section delivery of her child and what that had meant for her body. Reflecting on the physical and emotional accommodations she had to make in welcoming new life, she observes that she was stretching far beyond the previous physical boundaries her body had known pre-pregnancy. She was aware of the growing child pressing and pushing out the bounded contours of her heart and of the reality that, after one reaches out and embraces new life, one is never the same.

"After each birth, the body readjusts," she observes. "But things are never as they were before. Silverwebbed stretch marks are only an outward sign…Each child impresses upon waxen flesh the unique imprints of its life. Inscribes one's own life with an image all its own. Often I have thought how true that is of the heart itself."

How true that is of the heart itself! And so we're invited to reflect on how we've opened ourselves to God's justice journey, how we're learning to engage, with our whole heart, the values of the kingdom. The following suggestions invite us to further explore how we've been irrevocably marked.

Bodyprayer

Stand or sit in a comfortable position in a quiet place. Close your eyes. Imagine God's loving hospitality raining down over you. With your hands, touch your face and feel the blessing of this sacred shower.

Then imagine yourself and our entire world standing in that rain of God's love. No exceptions.

Scripture

Prayerfully read the parable of the Good Samaritan (Luke 10:25-37)

In reflecting on this familiar parable, Jon Sobrino[20] observes, "This meeting is where the human part is decided: Either you make a detour around him [the person who fell in with robbers], as the priest and the Levite of the parable did, or you heal his wounds."

What experiences have you had with the "stranger" that have invited you to be a healer of wounds?

Story

Read accounts of persons who opened themselves to acts of courage and generosity and stretched their worldview. The lives of the saints would be a good starting point.

In *St. Francis and the Foolishness of God*,[21] Marie Dennis recounts the story of St. Francis embracing a person afflicted with leprosy. She then offers this action:

> *"Let God lead you again to the 'leper'. Let the experience be a reflective one…a conscious and meditative move out from the familiar to the world of hurt… Allow the experience to challenge your assumptions about the margins."*

The arts

Reflect on a piece of art, listen to a piece of music, or read a poem created by an artist from a culture other than your own. Be attentive to what this feels like for you. Are there any learnings that come from your reflection?

Standing in a new place

Astronauts of many nations have experienced profound spiritual changes upon viewing the Earth from a new perspective: Space. From out in the universe, they witnessed our home, planet Earth, as fragile and wounded and beautiful, all at the same time. They experienced a newfound sense of tenderness for our planet and all who inhabit this sacred space.

Read about how this shift in seeing from a new place changed their worldview forever:
http://homepages.wmich.edu/~korista/astronauts.html

May our lives given over to God's justice journey continually reveal new stretch marks!

For Group Conversation and/or Journaling

Reflect on a situation in your life when you were invited to "stretch," to reach out to a person or persons very different from yourself or different from the corner of the world in which you felt comfortable.

Did you accept that invitation to grow?
If so, what did it feel like? If not, what held you back?

What other life experiences or events might have marked you with spiritual or cultural stretch marks?

How might God be inviting you to grow or to stretch at this time in your life?

Breathprayer

Sit in silence for several minutes at the close of this time.

As you become aware of your breathing, pray this mantra or one of your own choosing.

Breathing in: God embraces me.

Breathing out: I welcome the world.

Closing Prayer:

Journeying God,
move us beyond our comfort zone
to recognize you however and wherever you come
into our lives.
Stretch our sense
of what you look like, sound like, feel like.
Turn our fears to tears of compassion.
Engage us in fearless living.
Amen. Let it be so!

MAKING MYSTICAL SPACE

The Lavender Room at Sugar's Tea Room
This room is one of several welcoming spaces that offered an entry point into a gracious afternoon.

Breathprayer

Sit in a comfortable position in silence. As you become aware of your breathing, pray this mantra or one of your own choosing as you breathe in and out:

Breathing in: The Divine is here

Breathing out: and everywhere.

For Reflection

Space is so much more than a thing we occupy or fill up or even share. This entity is around us, above us, below us, within us, and at times, center stage in our awareness: when we start up a car to share the road; when we use mass transit and conform to the unwritten rules of respecting personal boundaries; when we experience the limits of space in a tiny apartment, a long checkout line, a crowded waiting room.

Robert Sardello has an unusual take on space, expressed in *Facing the World with Soul*.[22] He looks on space as an entity with which we are in partnership. Consequently, we're challenged to treat space with the same respect and reverence we would accord any partner. We must be in right relationship with space, and right relationship, as we know, is the definition of justice.

Sardello recalls a time when he was invited to speak to a group of city managers on the topic of architecture, to look at the ways architecture could enhance and improve the quality of city life. These managers were so focused on their task, their plans for renovating the city's architectural face, that they never noticed the face of the actual room in which they were meeting that day.

But Sardello did, and he was troubled. He remembers that, "The room itself was sick. It had no windows, and the drab acoustic ceilings pressed in from above, sandwiching the room with oppression. The door was without a handle...No molding marked a difference between ceilings and walls, walls and floor. Painted institutional gray, its floor covered with rough carpet, the space was filled with ugly brown folding chairs."

It was as if the room were crying out in pain, and Sardello was disturbed that not a single city manager seemed to notice the suffering of that space. As the discussion continued and focused on power and how the city managers would use power to effect change, Sardello questioned whether a work so important as the reshaping of the city could be entrusted to people who couldn't even recognize that the space in which they were gathered was itself hurting.

From Sardello's story, it seems that the way in which we relate to space is telling of our relationship with all creatures, living and inanimate, who share this planet with us. In this universe we inhabit, we need to reflect on how we define our space, what boundaries surround our space, who or what we invite to possess our space. What is in our consciousness of space reflects our values and reveals the essence of what is most precious to us.

In the United States, perhaps formed by westward expansion and the sense of a limitless frontier ("Don't Fence Me In"), some would define success in terms of possessing the largest space possible: building "McMansions"; erecting formidable walls and fences

designed to keep others out; forcing small
homeowners to abandon their space for the sake of
more and grander development; supersizing food;
"owning" natural resources, corporately or nationally.

Rather than the bigger-is-better philosophy, what if
we looked more deeply at the space of our lives in
terms of how to bless and make sacred what is already
there?

As we struggle to free ourselves of the false
burdens and false loyalties that can possess the space
of our hearts, why not start small, with perhaps a new
way of relating to space itself and to acknowledging
that it, too, is holy and created by God? This call to a
deepening awareness of space can be lived out in the
dailiness of our lives in simple and concrete ways.

Believing that the space where we work is sacred:

- We'll practice patience with technology (no
  easy task on some days!), praising the
  computer, copy machine, and other equipment
  when it works, and encouraging (imploring!
  begging!) it when it's stalled.
- We'll cultivate right speech when sending our
  words across the wider space of the telephone
  or Internet.
- We'll be careful of tone when expressing
  disagreement or frustration, showing respect
  for co-workers who inhabit space with us, and

showing respect for the memory of the space itself.

- We'll conserve energy and leave a light footprint, mindful that generations of others are counting on using this same space after us.
- We'll clean up any mental garbage—emotional burdens, attitudes of exclusion, and prejudices—before we enter our place of work and whenever we leave it.
- We'll create a place of beauty with small touches...a piece of art, a beloved photo, flowers.

Believing that the space where we live is sacred:

- We'll pray for protection for our home whenever we leave, and thank the space of our home for its hospitality when we return.
- We'll handle doors and windows—the threshold to our home—with reverence.
- We'll thank the plants who beautify our surroundings and purify the air we breathe.
- We'll recycle to preserve space for future generations and to create out of something used something new and life-giving.
- We'll put care and thought into what we choose to display on our walls and shelves.
- When we go into the kitchen to cook or to bake, we'll bless all who were involved in bringing the ingredients we use into our space: the earth which nurtured, the clouds that watered, the farmers who harvested, the workers who

packaged for production, the truckers who transported to market.

When the space of our hearts is possessed by God, when we struggle to live each moment in a state of mindfulness, our actions will be reflective of justice. This new and sometimes radical relationship with space frees us of clutter and invites us to more clearly and easily hear the Divine at work in our lives.

To get to that place, we're challenged to exorcise the demons—whatever they may be—that occupy the space of our hearts, and to replace them with God's concern for the healing of the universe. To get to that place, we're called to continually reflect on how our lives would be different if we lived in communion with, and in awareness of, space.

This, I believe, is what it means to fully inhabit the space of our lives, as Jesus did. This, I believe, is what it takes to make a mystic.

For Group Conversation and/or Journaling

Reflect on your own experience of space, especially personal space. Have you been in settings or situations where space or the lack of it became an awkward or difficult issue? Why?

How much space do you need to be comfortable? To feel safe?

Reflect on how space is viewed differently in cultures other than your own. What might be the learnings in that reflection?

"...we're challenged to exorcise the demons, whatever they may be, that occupy the space of our hearts and to replace them with God's concern for the healing of the universe."
How might you be called to widen the space of your heart to be fully inclusive?

Breathprayer

Sit in silence for several minutes at the close of this time.

As you become aware of your breathing, pray this mantra or one of your own choosing:

Breathing in: The Divine is here

Breathing out: and everywhere.

Closing Prayer:

God beyond boundaries,
there is room in your creation for all of us.
Widen the space of our hearts.
Open our minds.

*Stretch our attitudes
so that all may find in us a door to welcome and
acceptance.
Amen. Let it be so!*

BECOMING A "WE"

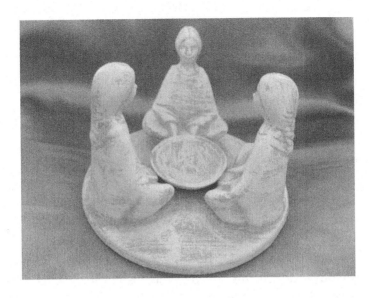

Three Women Sharing in a Circle
Pottery from Mexico

Breathprayer

Sit in a comfortable position in silence. As you
become aware of your breathing, pray this mantra
or one of your own choosing as you breathe in and
out:

Breathing in: God in me

Breathing out: And all of creation.

For Reflection

Mysticism and relationship converged the day the tulip tree died in our back yard. Over 80 feet tall, towering and solid, the tree seemed a magical companion to me, since she sprouted green "tulips" each spring. She was the keeper of my childhood secrets and the patient listener to my rambling imaginings.

One day, the old tulip tree, having faced too many seasons of heavy snow, fierce wind, and disease, was struck by lightning, splintering its huge branches. All through the following day, I heard the steady whine of the buzz saw cutting through the flesh of the injured tree. All day long I imagined—or did I?—my magical tree crying out in pain. When the cutting back and cutting away finally ended, I went out in the back yard to help clean up the debris. But mostly, I went out to console my friend and examine her wounds.

At one point in gathering up the fragments, I caught my finger on the rough edge of a branch and cut myself, my blood mingling with her sap. It occurred to me that the two elements are not all that different, as life forces go. I already knew intuitively that we were somehow related, that in some way the coming together of my blood and the tree's sap made us blood sisters, forming a pact that implied that we were in this together, that we would stand by one another no matter what. There were no words in my childhood vocabulary to describe this, but I believe it's what Barbara Brown Taylor in *An Altar in the World, A*

Geography of Faith, names as "bearing the reality of the universe in your flesh like a thorn."[23]

And just what is that reality? That our Earth is in pain, crying out like the wounded tulip tree. Crying out ultimately for healing and wholeness, but first and foremost for right relationship, an initial and critical step toward the healing of the whole. The call to healing our Earth is a call to communion, to understand that we are not separate nor apart from what wounds her, just as we're not distant from what restores her vitality and richness. It's a call to continually examine our pronouns, relating to Earth as a "she," a vibrant mother, rather than an "it," a thing to be used or abused to suit our own purposes.

Marilou Awiakta expresses this relationship and the implications of disregarding it, in her poem, "When Earth Becomes an 'It'":[24]

When the people call Earth "Mother,"
they take with love
and with love give back
so that all may live.

When the people call Earth "it,"
they use her
consume her strength.
Then the people die.

Already the sun is hot
out of season.
Our mother's breast

is going dry.
She is taking all green
into her heart
and will not turn back
until we call her
by her name.

How we name ourselves and all of creation has much to say about how we relate to one another. The movement towards healing the Earth comes about in a paradigm shift where we no longer see our survival or our thriving as in any way separate from that of our Earth. Wesley Granberg-Michaelson, in "Renewing the Whole Creation,"[25] calls on us to examine our theology of relationship in regard to the Earth, defining three possible ways of relating:

- Dominion (assuming that humanity's God-given duty is to exploit the Earth in meeting any needs and fulfilling any desires)
- Stewardship (stressing humanity's obligation to be a wise caretaker of the Earth; this still implies a managerial relationship to Nature. Humanity's task is to govern and order Nature wisely, like a good monarch)
- Interrelationship (seeing that creation has value because of its relationship to God, rather than its utility for humanity)

Clearly, the healing of our Earth, the healing of ourselves, is bound up with living from the third theology of interelationship, one that will save us all both now and into future generations.

I was taken back to the day the tulip tree died in reading "For All My Relations" by George Tinker.[26] He relates a blessing ceremony where Native Americans formed a circle around a tree that was about to be cut down, speaking prayers and uttering words of comfort to the tree. Those gathered also made an offering to the Creator as a way of maintaining the harmony and balance of creation even as an act of violence (cutting down the tree) was about to be enacted. Tinker asks, "What sort of reciprocity do we engage in, will we engage in? What do we return to the Earth when we clear cut a forest or strip mine, leaving miles upon miles of Earth totally bare? Perhaps more painfully, the same question can be put in terms of human justice: where is the reciprocity, the maintaining of cosmic balance, with respect to those who are suffering varieties of oppression in our modern world?"

Tinker emphasizes the Lakota phrase, *Mitakuye oyasin,* "For all my relations," to show the centrality of creation. Our relations, our relatives, must necessarily include the four-leggeds, the wingeds, and all the living-moving things on Mother Earth. So we aren't the only ones doing the naming! I like to imagine that our four-legged and winged relatives and all the "above-me and below-me and around-me" beings have already chosen names for us. What will those names reveal about who we are?

Mitakuye oyasin. The heart of the matter is interrelatedness and interdependence, balance and relationship. The hour is upon us to see ourselves as one with all creation. The hour is upon us to make the movement from living as an "I" to becoming a "We," for the sake of all our relations, for the healing of our Earth.

For Group Conversation and/or Journaling

Mitakuye oyasin. For all my relations. Who or what does this include in your life? To which relations in the natural world are you most drawn?

Wesley Granberg-Michaelson describes three ways of relating to Earth: dominion, stewardship, and interrelationship. Where do you stand in this theology of relationship?

Might our efforts for the healing of Mother Earth also effect our own healing? In what ways?

Breathprayer

Sit in silence for several minutes at the close of this time.

As you become aware of your breathing, pray this mantra or one of your own choosing as you breathe in and out:

Breathing in: God in me

Breathing out: And all of creation.

Closing Prayer:

Creating God,
you look with love
on all that walks,
swims, crawls,
grows green in our world.
Lead us to deeper relationship
and respect
for our Mother Earth
and all our relations.
Heal our common wounds
and bring us to wholeness,
the fullness of your dream for all creation.
Amen. Let it be so.

TAKING IT PERSONALLY

Broken Pot on Kitchen Floor

Breathprayer

Sit in a comfortable position in silence. As you become aware of your breathing, pray this mantra or one of your own choosing as you breathe in and out:

Breathing in: My heart is broken wide.

Breathing out: My heart is open to God.

For Reflection

Many years ago, I was part of a group of dedicated activists gathered for a planning process. At the beginning of the session, each of us was asked to name a particular gift that we brought to this meeting. A litany of wonderful attributes followed as people named their gifts: hospitality, generosity, a sense of humor, commitment, and so on. I was comfortably settled into this lovely affirmation of the qualities of those gathered when suddenly one person added, "Brokenness. I bring the gift of my brokenness."

I sat bolt upright. Until that moment, I don't think I had ever thought of brokenness as something positive, much less a gift. But in the years since, I've come to see brokenness as exactly that—a gift—a gift that invites us to reflect on how we've contributed to the wounds of our world; a gift that opens us to live with compassion for another's reality; a gift that challenges us to make justice personal.

As a writer, I find it incredibly easy to dash off a response supporting or opposing a justice issue. Today that's a process made especially easy by the many faith-based organizations providing ready-made letters to which a personal message can be added online. Yet I also believe that writing that letter or signing that petition or making that phone call—as critical and important as that action is—can't be the end, the final response. To effect change in ourselves as well as change in the structures and policies that wound our world, we need to bring those same issues to our contemplation and reflection. We need to make them deeply personal in the way that Julia Esquivel describes:

> *When it is necessary to drink so much pain,*
> *When a river of anguish*
> *drowns us,*
> *When we have wept many tears*
> *and they flow like rivers*
> *from our sad eyes,*
> *Only then*
> *does the deep hidden sigh of our neighbor*
> *become our own.*
> *("The Sigh" from* The Certainty of Spring)[27]

When we take the deep, hidden sigh of our neighbor into our heart, we're taking justice personally. Many of the people who have become dear friends in my parish community in southeast Queens have experienced first-hand discrimination, racism, exclusion from places of power and decision-making.

Though, sadly, their experience is not uncommon in our society, what is exceptional is the way in which these dear friends have integrated profoundly painful life experiences into their worldview, and how they've refused—emphatically refused—to let brokenness embitter or defeat them. Instead, they've turned every negative experience on its head!

Reflecting on their own suffering and the deep hidden sigh of their neighbor has fueled their determination to insure that no one, no sister or

brother here at home or anywhere in our world, is
ever again oppressed or marginalized. This is what
impels them to work tirelessly for a more just,
inclusive world, for the fulfillment of Dr. King's dream
of the beloved community. This is what happens when
a community or an individual takes justice very
personally.

In the company of so many shining lights, we're
invited to keep learning life's big lessons: to draw
deeper compassion from our own brokenness, to
imagine ourselves in other people's lives, and to keep
on asking:

- How does it feel to be broken by homelessness,
  living on the streets, never getting a good
  night's sleep because we have to guard both
  our body from harm and our few possessions
  from theft?
- What is it like to be broken by violence in our
  neighborhood, shaken awake at night by
  gunfire and gangs and kept awake in fear for
  our children's safety and our utter
  powerlessness to ever completely protect them,
  much as we long to?
- What does it mean to be broken by an
  impossible economic system, weighed down
  by foreclosure or unscrupulous mortgage
  practices that threaten to tear away from our
  family the only home we've ever known?
- How does it feel to live within the boundaries
  of our broken immigration policy, always alert

to the threat of raids and deportation, always sensitive to a climate of unwelcome, always exhausted by the backbreaking work which is all that's available to us because we have no documents to prove we "belong"?

On the deepest, most profound level, we need to take the brokenness that is part of our human condition personally. We need to put a human face on the issues of our time. Otherwise, they remain simply issues—they are "out there," a statistic to be addressed and a point from which to move on. If we keep the issues distant from our hearts, nothing significant is demanded of us; nothing challenges us to be radically transformed. Justice doesn't get personal.

But it must. Elizabeth O'Connor in *The New Community*[28] notes that the mark of a liberating community, which is what we aspire to belong to, is "a clear, radical, unequivocal commitment to the poorest, the weakest, and the most abused members of the human family." In other words, to the broken.

This unequivocal commitment to those who are broken was dramatically underscored in a presentation, "Genocide: Can Love Prevail?" at Maryknoll.[29] One of the speakers was Dativa Nyangezi Ngaboyisana, a Rwandan, a genocide survivor, and now a warden at the 6,000 inmate prison in the capital, Kigali. In the prison where she works as a warden, more than half of the women and men inmates have been convicted of perpetrating crimes against humanity during the same Rwandan genocide which Dativa survived.

How could she, a survivor, turn around and minister to the very people who had brutalized both her and so many she had loved and lost? With a stunning largeness of heart, Dativa observed of those who had participated in the genocide, "Because these people have committed such atrocious crimes, they have to be treated with a lot of love so they can be transformed."

As we struggle to learn from our own brokenness and to be moved to compassion by the brokenness of our world, let us also continue to be inspired by the great cloud of witnesses who intuitively know that, for them, there is no way to justice except to take it personally.

For Group Conversation and/or Journaling

Reflect on a time when you or someone you cared for experienced or witnessed the challenges of homelessness or violence or poverty or immigration. How did you respond or react? What learnings were there for you in such an experience?

In speaking of those who participated in the Rwandan genocide, Dativa Nyangezi Ngaboyisana remarked, "Because these people have committed such atrocious crimes, they have to be treated with a lot of love so they can be transformed." What moves within you when you hear that statement?

"This is what happens when a community or individual takes justice very personally." What do you think happens when this is in place?

What issues of social justice draw you or touch your life on a personal level?

In what ways might your own/your nation's lifestyle or choices contribute to the brokenness of our world?

Breathprayer

Sit in silence for several minutes at the close of this time.

As you become aware of your breathing, pray this mantra or one of your own choosing as you breathe in and out:

Breathing in: My heart is broken wide.

Breathing out: My heart is open to God.

Closing Prayer:

Wounded God,
you see our pain

and know our anguish.
As we struggle with the brokenness of the human
family
and our own wounds of selfishness, fear, or
division,
we pray:
Make us whole.
Make us whole.
Make us whole.
Amen. Let it be so.

CASTING A WIDER NET

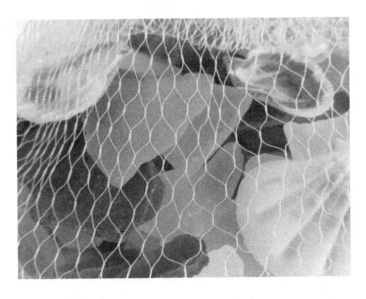

An Offering from the Sea
Sea glass and shells gathered from the shore in New Jersey

Breathprayer

Sit in a comfortable position in silence. As you become aware of your breathing, pray this mantra or one of your own choosing as you breathe in and out:

Breathing in: My heart is open

Breathing out: to all God loves.

For Reflection

It was one of my favorite rituals of summer: sitting near the bulkhead and watching my nieces and nephews in the waters outside my parents' home in Point Pleasant Beach. Here the seining net, a long, rectangular piece of fishing net with a pole at either end, was always a favorite attraction.

Two children would each hold one of the poles, moving further and further apart to stretch it out into a straight line. Then, with great care, they'd walk toward each other to form a closed circle. Their goal was to be as open as possible, to invite the greatest number of sea creatures to enter the embrace of the net. It was a skill honed by trial and error. If they moved too slowly, crabs, small fish, and other treasures would be gone. Too quickly, and they'd have an empty circle as well.

Over time, as my nieces and nephews became more practiced, they learned a valuable truth: the wider the circle, the greater the haul. And so, as their seining expertise deepened, their net widened. They'd each hold an end, move outward, then come together to complete the circle. Hauling the seine net ashore, they'd stand back, eyes wide with excitement, while the net gave up its treasures.

Like many rituals of childhood, the seine net was about more than play. "Everything that happens to you is your teacher," notes Polly Berrien. "The secret is to learn to sit at the feet of your life and be taught."

Over time and with reflection on experience, those who work with seine nets learn life's big lessons: Cast a wider net. Leave nothing out. Look at the consequences of every act. Learn from the struggle to be inclusive. Don't go it alone. Be supported by a partner or a group. Form community.

I believe the seine net also has something to say to us in our struggles to shape a more just, inclusive world:

Cast a wider net in praying

> Widen the space of your net by adding to your intercessory prayers each day people you might not ordinarily include. Listen to the news of the day and pray for someone who seems to be outside the realm of others' prayers...a person who holds a position or viewpoint in absolute opposition to yours, a person whose violent acts make him appear beyond redemption. Try praying with love and compassion for someone you'd usually consider beyond the circle of your prayers' embrace.

Cast a wider net in language

> Be conscious of using inclusive language in prayer, in conversation, in thought. Because language structures thought, if something is not in your language, it's usually not in your consciousness. Because of this, be especially aware that the language you use is inclusive,

not leaving out any group based on gender,
sexual orientation, class, culture, race. Avoid
stereotypes and labeling, which diminish your
own circle of welcome.

Cast a wider net in image and symbol

Bring into your home art and artifacts from
cultures other than your own. Read the poetry
of many nations. Invite the wisdom of Jewish,
Buddhist, Sufi, Christian and other traditions
into your reflections. Reflect on how this
practice influences your imagination of the
divine and your sense of God at work in the
universe.

Cast a wider net in attitudes

A spiritual leader once suggested what she
called "benevolent glancing," meaning that
each time you see any person, you pray, "I
wish for you all good." Send thoughts of
welcome and affirmation to everyone you meet
in the course of a day. From attitudes flow
actions, so work to make your attitudes those
of unconditional welcome.

Cast a wider net in associations

Cultivate the openness of heart needed to
welcome into the circle of your life those who
may stretch your worldview and redefine your
boundaries. Invite the great cloud of witnesses,
the communion of saints—both those living

among us and those who have gone before us—into your company. When you stand with these holy ones, you cannot look at the realities of our world with indifference. The circles of your life will forever expand.

It's quite simple, really. It's Seine Net 101, beckoning us to life's big lessons. Leave nothing out. Learn to invite. Cast a wider net. Live in the image of our God who embraces all.

For Group Conversation and/or Journaling

The faith-praxis cycle always begins with tapping into one's own life experience on an issue. As you reflect on circles of inclusion, recall an experience where you were excluded from an activity or an event, or were left "out of the loop." Revisit those feelings of exclusion or alienation and reflect on what you wished you could have done to change your situation.

Or recall a time when a group of which you were part excluded others from membership. How did that make you feel? How did it alter your feelings about belonging to that particular group?

Dr. Martin Luther King noted that, "In a real sense, all life is interrelated. All people are caught in an inescapable network of mutuality, tied in a single garment of destiny."[30]

Whom do you consider to be in the "net" with you?
Are there others to whom you might be reluctant to
extend a welcome? Reflect on any conditions you may
be putting on belonging.

Breathprayer

Sit in silence for several minutes at the close of this
time.

As you become aware of your breathing, pray this
mantra or one of your own choosing as you
breathe in and out:

Breathing in: My heart is open

Breathing out: to all God loves.

Closing Prayer:

Welcoming God,
you are so much bigger
than our imagination.
You bless our world
without exception.
Open our hearts
to new ways
of being, of doing.
Lead us to celebrate
the many reflections
of your face

in our sisters and brothers
wherever and however
we find them.
Amen. Let it be so!

EMBODYING JUSTICE

Bust of Ballerina
This statue was created by the artist, Cipriano

Breathprayer

Sit in a comfortable position in silence. As you become aware of your breathing, pray this mantra or one of your own choosing as you breathe in and out:

Breathing in: With God in the darkness

Breathing out: I stay.

For Reflection

The body is the keeper of memory, holding a record of pain, ecstasy, wounds and dreams.

I'm reminded of a time in my life when, because of an accident, I lived in my body with something that I can only call terror. For three years, I continued to be a capable, creative, even presence in my professional work, because I had no time to dwell on anything but the projects in front of me. But in the unguarded, unstructured moments of late night, I would fall asleep, then awake soon after with shallow breath, palpitations, anxiety, followed by a long night of "what if's." My imagination, a gift I've always treasured, became something of a demon in those endless hours, as it raced through every possible outcome. The stress was so constant and so intense that I feared a heart attack was imminent.

I wanted desperately to run away, to escape. I just wanted it to be over, to live apart from such a terrible space. And so, every morning, I invited my body into a ritual where I blessed it and begged its forgiveness for the burden it had to carry. Eventually, the situation was resolved, but my body has not forgotten. And it has taught me lessons that could not be learned any other way except by being in a place of such pain.

On the deepest intuitive level, I learned that my experience was part of the wounding of the cosmos, and that it was calling forth a cosmic embrace of comfort and healing from strangers I had never met. I learned great compassion for all those who at the same moment also experienced suffering, and surely to a much greater degree than I. I learned most of all the great value of staying with the pain, learning from it, not living in front of it or alongside of it, but living smack in the middle of it. I learned that transformation cannot happen without faithfulness.

"Faithfulness," Robert Wicks notes, "opens the door to the insight that it is not the amount of darkness in the world or in us that is crucial. In the end, it is how we stand in that darkness that really matters. Moreover, sometimes it is paradoxically during faithfulness in the darkness, not in the light, that we may see what is true and dear at a deeper level….When we cry out in prayer amidst the darkness, the very circumstances that are so oppressive to us begin to create something new…"[31]

This may just be the critical issue to consider as we struggle to embody justice: how to live a life that is faithful; how to live our belief that present realities— as seemingly tragic and hopeless as they appear—are not ultimate, are not the last word.

Surely our bodies have something to teach us here. We know from the studies of Jean Piaget that the body is our earliest classroom. Before we ever speak or understand words, we come to know the world around us through our bodies, through touching, tasting, shaking, falling. Why, then, should we not let our body, with all its wounds, dreams, revelations, and memory, continue to teach us to embody justice later in life?

"In our bodies, in this moment, there live the seed impulses of the change and spiritual growth we seek, and to awaken them we must bring our awareness into the body, into the here and now," claims Pat Ogden in *Discovering the Body's Wisdom*.

Marching with Dr. Martin Luther King, Jr. in Alabama, Abraham Heschel declared, "My feet were praying."[32] Perhaps in those times when words fail us, when we are struggling to move an issue forward, we need to embody gestures of movement—walking, running, dancing, throwing off obstacles—so that our bodies can move us into the place where our imagination dreams we can be.

We embody justice when we link hands together against injustice; when we stand for hours in demonstrations and peaceful protests; when we hug children; when we sit at the bedside of a loved one; when we engage in ministry; when we model, in the way we live, the Gospel values that sustain us.

Perhaps most significantly, we embody justice when we stay faithful for the long haul, as Nelson Mandela did through over 25 years of brutal confinement on Robben Island; as the civil rights activists did through ridicule and imprisonment; as countless unnamed and unheralded people do in struggling to make our world more just and inclusive. To create and initiate are relatively easy; to follow-up and sustain momentum for the long haul requires *hypomene*: "patient endurance, the ability to be poised to do what is needed even though all the going seems to be against one."[33]

To effect this, we need to be not observers, but participants in the sense that Barbara Kingsolver describes in *Animal Dreams*: "Here's what I've decided: the very least you can do is figure out what you hope for. And the most you can do is live inside that hope. Not admire it from a distance, but live right in it, under its roof."[34]

Thomas Cullinan, OSB, notes that, "Staying power is a quality we need very badly and that very few people have. They seem to lack long-term courage, that creative patience—not the sort of patience that is basically a sort of apathy, but the sort of patience that knows how to go on and on until the end appears—to hang on to the vision until it is possible to be creative with it, and not to give up one's vision just because things seem to be hopeless."[35]

In our struggle to embody justice, we are called to have this kind of staying power, to immerse ourselves in the struggle rather than watch it from a distance. We need to come to what the blind French resistance fighter Jacques Lusseyran calls "an end to living in front of things and a beginning of living with them." "This," he insists, "is love."[36] This is the embodiment of justice.

For Group Conversation and/or Journaling

Recall an emotionally or physically painful experience that your body has not forgotten. What was the challenge for you in staying with the pain? What were your learnings? Who or what enabled you to keep hope alive?

Marching with Dr. Martin Luther King, Jr., Abraham Heschel declared, "My feet were praying." When and where have your feet been praying?

Robert Wicks notes that, "When we cry out in prayer amidst the darkness, the very circumstances that are so oppressive to us begin to create something new." What is the something new that might be created?

Breathprayer

Sit in silence for several minutes at the close of this time.

As you become aware of your breathing, pray this mantra or one of your own choosing as you breathe in and out:

Breathing in: With God in the darkness

Breathing out: I stay.

Closing prayer

Staying God,
staying with us
in our darkness,
in our doubt,
in our anguish,
in our despair.
Hold on to our hope.
Enlighten our learnings.
Shore up our passion.
Remain,
remain,
remain
among us
always and forever.
Amen. Let it be so.

LIVING ON THE BRIDGE

Bridge over the Lackawanna River
Near the Heritage Trail in Carbondale, Pennsylvania, this area provides one of my favorite spots for walking.

Breathprayer

Sit in a comfortable position in silence. As you become aware of your breathing, pray this mantra or one of your own choosing as you breathe in and out:

Breathing in: Who is my neighbor?

Breathing out: God is here.

For Reflection

This is a story of transition, yours, mine and ours, for we are all sojourners.

Many years ago, my father began a long journey of dialysis treatments. And every week, after visiting him and kissing him good-bye, I'd leave the hospital overwhelmed at how illness had ravaged this man I loved. Somehow I'd manage to contain my heartache until I boarded the train for the long ride from the Jersey shore back to Long Island.

Once slumped in my seat, I'd begin my grieving: let out a long, slow sigh, heavy with all I'd just taken in, and then a quiet trickle of tears to mourn the little deaths I had witnessed that day.

And every Sunday, as I wept for my Dad, the conductor on that NJ Transit train had his own ritual. He would punch my ticket, take note of my red eyes, and put his hand on my shoulder. No words were spoken, but always there was the human touch of compassion from someone who had no idea what my sorrow was, only that it was.

To this day, I can feel the comfort of the conductor's hand. Such a simple gesture, really, but such a grand one. It connected me to the human community and to our common struggle with transition. It said to me, "You are not alone. Whatever your sadness, you are not without power. You will get through this; in fact, you will do more than survive: you will flourish."

Fast forward many years later. Once again it's a Sunday and I'm saying good-bye. Once again feelings of powerlessness and sadness overwhelm. Only this time, I'm in a place where even the simple consolation of a human touch is denied.

I'm standing in the Refugee Detention Center in Elizabeth, NJ. This windowless converted warehouse, a non-criminal facility in an industrial section, holds several hundred undocumented persons. From the visitors' side of the glass, I can hear Creole, Spanish, Chinese, Arabic, French, and some languages I can't identify, spoken into telephones to loved ones on the other side. All around me are the devastating effects of living in this constant state of transition: the quiet tears, the brave smiles, the hands held up to the glass partition—the nearest thing to human touch offered by wives, husbands, partners, parents, children, friends, advocates.

Many of the refugees detained here came to the U.S. fleeing persecution, leaving their homeland in fear for their lives. They arrived in the U.S. without a valid visa or passport or other documentation. Instead of moving into a haven of welcome and freedom from persecution, they entered the limbo of not knowing, a place of loneliness, waiting, uncertainty that is the fate of detainees.

Laurie E. O'Bryon, in *The Mustard Seed*, a publication of Jesuit Refugee Service/USA[37] notes:

"There is an increasing tendency in both the United States and overseas to place people who are seeking political asylum in detention facilities or prisons while their cases are being adjudicated. These are people who are seeking protection from persecution, yet they are greeted with the prospect of months (or longer) in prison or prison-like facilities. Asylum seekers are not criminals; they have a right under international law to cross borders to seek protection."

More than that, they have a right to safe passage and welcome based on the Biblical mandate found in Leviticus:

> *"Do not mistreat foreigners who are living in your land. Love them as you love yourselves. Remember that you, too, were once foreigners." (Leviticus 19:33)*

These refugees may request political asylum in the U.S. and file a fear of persecution claim. They may be transported to immigration detention, where eventually a credible fear interview is arranged; if credible fear is established, they may be detained and wait for a hearing before an immigration judge on their asylum claim. If their claim is denied, a removal order may be issued or an appeal may be filed, in which case they'll continue waiting in detention. For the lucky ones, asylum may eventually be granted after months or years of waiting. But regardless of the outcome, the element common to all refugees detained is the waiting, the living in a chronic state of transition.

"Most of the world's nations have ratified the 1951 United Nations Convention Relating to the Status of Refugees," notes O'Bryon, "and, as such, have agreed to accept and protect refugees fleeing persecution. Yet, who would define 'protection' as including incarceration?"

Refugees are living the shadow side of the Celtic image of "edges." The edges are places of transition, mystery, interfaces between this world and the next, spaces of great risk, danger and potential. In the Celtic world, the edges where sea meets shore, sky meets land, the turning point of day to night or one year to the next, the areas marked by bridges, stairways, crossroads—all of these edges are rich with meaning and truly liminal. But for refugees in detention, the edges mean something else:

"The unknown duration, reasons and outcome of detention are particularly stressful for detainees. It renders them hopeless and helpless. They cannot pace themselves through a fixed period of time. They face the threat of transfer to another detention location, the fear of deportation, and the constant hope of release," observes Dr. Christina Pourgourides.[38]

It's one thing to approach living on the edges by choice, coming from a stance of privilege with other options and safety nets lined up just in case things don't work out. It's quite another experience to live on the edges as detainees do, to see no way out, no hope in sight.

Alby Stone in *The Perilous Bridge* describes one of the edges, a bridge, as "a structure that joins two otherwise separate pieces of land, yet at the same time enhances their separateness. One can travel across it, from one land mass to another, *but while on it, the traveller is neither in one place nor the other.*"[39] For vulnerable refugees, the experience of the edges is not of crossing the bridge but of having to live on the bridge in a constant state of transition. Though the challenge of crossing such a bridge is considerable, being detained on it indefinitely, being neither here nor there, neither one place nor another, is far more demoralizing.

Jesuit Refugee Service-NJ circulated a flyer seeking volunteers from northern New Jersey to companion asylum seekers detained in the Elizabeth Detention Center. The flyer's stark invitation read:

"Your new neighbor
lives somewhere with
no windows
no phone calls
and no exits.
Let them know that someone cares:
Visit a refugee in immigration detention."

Our new neighbor is living on the bridge. Our new neighbor asks only for what we all desire: safe passage and a lasting home. Isn't it time we crossed this bridge together?

For Group Conversation and/or Journaling

What is the immigrant history of your family? What were their hopes and dreams when they departed from their country of origin? How were they received upon arriving in a foreign land?

Reflect on a time in your life when you were in pain and someone comforted you, or when you offered this presence to another. Even if this support couldn't change the circumstances causing suffering, what did such solidarity offer?

How do you define "neighbor"? Are there individuals or groups you would find it difficult to include in this definition? Who? Why? What does the witness of Gospel inclusion challenge you to do?

Breathprayer

Sit in silence for several minutes at the close of this time.

As you become aware of your breathing, pray this mantra or one of your own choosing as you breathe in and out:

Breathing in: Who is my neighbor?

Breathing out: God is here.

Closing Prayer:

Journeying God,
accompany those who are on the move:
uprooted,
exiled,
detained,
seeking safe passage.
Open our hearts
and urge us to advocate for those in need
so that all people
may find a secure and lasting home.
Amen. Let it be so.

WORKING FROM OUR HEARTS
INTO OUR HANDS

Breathprayer

Sit in a comfortable position in silence. As you become aware of your breathing, pray this mantra or one of your own choosing as you breathe in and out:

Breathing in: My mission

Breathing out: To spend myself in love.

For Reflection

It was one of those Kodak moments, forever preserved in memory and frozen in time, and it delights me still.

While traveling in Ireland, I was with a group that stopped to see a demonstration of sheep-herding. At the top of a mountain grazed five sheep, small as dots, while our group waited below. We listened intently as the shepherd explained how his dogs, Border Collies, were trained to follow both the spoken and whistled commands of stop, wait, left, and right. The dogs were never given rewards for a job well done, the shepherd explained. No rewards were needed, for the work itself was its own reward.

Most of this would have made only a slight impression on me were it not for the youngest Border Collie that was part of the demonstration. At the mere hint that this pup might be pressed into service, his eyes blazed with excitement. As the shepherd talked, the dog leaped up and down over and over, as if to say, "Here I am! I'm ready! I'm willing! Send me! Please, please, please!" His whole demeanor shouted that this was the work he was born for, that he couldn't wait for the moment of fulfillment. Once the command was given, the Collie tore off to the mountaintop, followed the shepherd's commands flawlessly, and returned the herd to the bottom, barely panting and full of eagerness to begin again.

My delight in remembering that image lingers still, as fresh as it was at the foot of the green Irish hills. That little Border Collie made the words of the Buddha come alive:

"Your work is to discover your world and then with all your heart, give yourself to it."[40]

I so much wanted to chat with that little Collie, to tap into his enthusiasm as he entered wholeheartedly and with abandon into his work in the world. In some mysterious way, he speaks to me still about working, and working for justice.

If we apply the Buddha's mandate to justice work, then there is nothing part-time about "discovering our world, and giving ourselves over to it." This is the work of a lifetime, not a selective picking and choosing when it's convenient, when we have the time or the energy. No, the mandate is quite clear: Our work is to discover our world, and then to give ourselves to it. Wholeheartedly. Full-time.

I suspect that a continual working for justice is not as complicated as we sometimes believe. We know that social justice calls us to walk on the "two feet" of charity and advocacy. Charity, or direct service, assists people in their immediate need, such as feeding the hungry in soup kitchens and offering a safe place to stay in homeless shelters. Advocacy addresses the root causes of social ills and works to effect changes in the systems and structures that oppress people by lobbying, demonstrating, protesting, and other actions. These two feet of charity and advocacy enable the human family to move forward.

But the mandate on work, "to discover our world and then, with all our heart, to give ourselves to it," can be accomplished not only when we're engaged in direct service or advocacy, but at every moment of our everyday living. *The Church in the Modern World*[41] noted that, "One of the gravest errors of our time is the dichotomy between the faith which many profess, and their day-to-day conduct." Do we make the connection that we are living our faith and engaged in spirituality not only when we're formally praying, but all through the day? Surely this is what the U.S. Bishops suggested in *Everyday Christianity*,[42] when they invited us to see our lives from a divine perspective, working to bring all that we are and all that we do in accord with God's will for building a community of justice, mercy, love and peace. Definitely not part-time work!

When we're being an active and concerned participant in Church or neighborhood activities, when we're carpooling, praying, cooking dinner, working at a job that supports our family or community, what is the divine perspective? What does God see when God looks at our jobs, family life, relationships, leisure, how we live the everyday in relationship to the larger community? Are we trying, in those ordinary moments and experiences, to bring the gospel values of compassion, nonviolence, integrity, and stewardship to the task at hand? If so, we're truly doing the work of justice, we're seeing our entire lives as an arena for social justice. We're witnessing that social justice is about right relationship to God, to ourselves, to one another, to all of creation.

In Austria, there is a wonderful custom of greeting people with the words, *"Gruss Gott."* When people exchange it, they are greeting God, acknowledging God present in the other and in that moment. It affirms that no part of our lives is too small to offer insight into the web of relationships that is at the heart of justice work. We live lives of everyday choices, all of them having an impact on the rest of the world. What we buy, what we eat, what we wear, what we labor at, how we spend leisure, with whom we share time and love–all of these are ways of greeting God.

And nothing is too insignificant to contribute to a more just, inclusive world. Brenda Paterson tells us that, "When we clean up after ourselves, whether it's a spilled jar, a broken chair, a disorganized study, or a death, we can see and reflect upon our own life and perhaps envision a way that won't be so broken, so violent, so unconscious. By cleaning up our own homes we take responsibility for ourselves and for preserving what we love."[43]

And when we give ourselves over to this work with our whole heart, we are in good company, not working alone, but in partnership with God and the whole human family. In *A Benedictine Spirituality of*

Work, Norvene Vest observes that, "The 'work' of the reconciliation of the world to God and of the transformation of all things into their intended fullness in Christ is in part *our* work, no less than God's."[44] Human work, she contends, is a primary means of caring for the world God has given us.

This is our work for justice, as well as the vocation of daily life: engaging in God's dream of building a community of justice, mercy, love and peace. In this work, attitudes are converted. We ourselves become more loving and just. The changes we make in our lives affect not only personal relationships, but also social relationships, structures and systems. By just such work is our world transformed, as in Brian Andreas' dream:

> *... the angel shrugged and said,*
> *If we fail this time,*
> *it will be a failure of the imagination.*
> *And then she placed the world softly in the palm of*
> *my hand.*[45]

May imagination not fail us.
May passion surround us.
May God's grace accompany the work of our hands and heart.

For Group Conversation and/or Journaling

What is the work for which you were born, the work for which you came into this world? Is this any different from your day-to-day work?

The Buddha says that your work is "to discover your world and then with all your heart give yourself to it." What are some of the things which might help you to fully discover your work in the world?

We live lives of everyday choices, all of them having an impact on the rest of the world. How do your choices connect to the broader sense of mission, of being sent?

Breathprayer

Sit in silence for several minutes at the close of this time.

As you become aware of your breathing, pray this mantra or one of your own choosing as you breathe in and out:

Breathing in: My mission

Breathing out: To spend myself in love.

Closing Prayer:

Working God,
you embraced your mission,
your work in this world.
We, too, are sent
by your grace
to work for justice
in the arena of our daily living.
May our every choice
bear witness to the common good
and to your loving care
for our sisters and brothers
everywhere.
Amen. Let it be so.

MIDWIFING RECONCILIATION

Offering the Bread of Justice
Photograph of a friend's hands, Christ the King parish,
Springfield Gardens, New York

Breathprayer

Sit in a comfortable position in silence. As you
become aware of your breathing, pray this mantra
or one of your own choosing as you breathe in and
out:

Breathing in: In the heart of God,

Breathing out: We are all found.

For Reflection

This world holds endless opportunities for
reconciliation, and some of my favorites reveal
themselves in the kitchen. I turn on the lights and bless
the space. I draw in all those for whom my hands will
knead the dough or mix the batter. I call the spices by
name and reverence the flour and sugar, the eggs and
butter, as well as the hands and hearts that have
carried them from farm and garden into my home.

I don't come into the kitchen to bake. I come to
have a conversation, to reconcile myself with the
elements of my world, to put things right in this
microcosm. When I bake, I take on the role of midwife,
ushering the ingredients into a new way of being. And
I long for all people, for all creation, to have what is
here at this moment in the kitchen.

In my baking is a prayer for reconciliation. In my
baking, I can taste the courage of Nelson Mandela,
returning to face his captors on Robben Island,
wanting to usher justice and reconciliation into the
new millennium; I savor the quiet dignity of Dr.
Martin Luther King, Jr., nonviolently meeting racial
bias with a refusal to back down from his quest for
equal justice for all people.

I've no idea if Mr. Mandela or Dr. King were bakers
like me, but I do know they were definitely midwives.
A strange and startling title, perhaps, for these
witnesses who happen to be men. But I believe that in
the struggle for justice—which is ultimately the

struggle to restore and maintain right relationship—they must be called midwives. Midwives who, in the midst of conflict and uncertainty, remained faithful to the difficult task of staying with the process of reconciliation. Midwives who brokered new understandings and worldviews, both cosmic and microcosmic. And though Mandela and King and the great cloud of witnesses are remembered for the largeness of their hearts and the extraordinary scope of their reconciliation, they learned and practiced this midwifery in the sometimes small, sometimes ordinary challenges of the everyday.

The midwife is charged with bringing life into this world. She [I use the feminine pronoun, but include all people here] enters a place fraught with both danger and possibility. Though her focus is on life and protecting and accompanying that life to a healthy emergence, she does this by planting herself in the midst of a process that is bloody, messy, and bordering on death. She does this by being relational to all involved in the process: coaching mother and father, coaxing out the fragile new life that is in the in-between time.

Christin Lore Weber in *Blessings, A WomanChrist Reflection on the Beatitudes*,[46] notes that the role of the midwife is to enter the lost places with her who will give birth. What are these lost places? On a microcosmic scale, they are the places of words thrown in anger, never able to be taken back. The places of hearts hardened by grudges. The places

where fear or woundedness has cut off compassion.
The places where deep listening has not been an
option. On a cosmic scale, they are the places of war,
genocide, regional conflicts, the wounding of the
universe.

English poet William Blake claims that the ability to
enter the lost places is a powerful witness to the
Incarnation. He cites the capacity of Jesus to forgive
another and to reenter vulnerably into the deepest
relation with another as the strongest evidence of
Jesus' being God in the flesh.[47] Those caught in the lost
places were so dear to Jesus' heart that he wrapped
them in parables, and named them as the lost coin, the
lost sheep, the lost son. And he indicated that the
search for the lost—our work for reconciliation—is
both a mandate and an extravagance. Ninety-nine are
left in the search for the lost sheep. An entire house is
swept in the quest for the lost coin. A wasted legacy is
forgotten in the welcome home of the lost son.

These lost places are any areas of both our personal
and global lives that cry for reconciliation with
ourselves, with others, or with all of creation. To enter
and restore these lost places, we must also be
midwives. Our entire focus, our full energy, must be
on two actions: letting go and coming through. Letting
go frees the energy we've formerly trapped by holding
grudges, nursing wounds, or closing hearts. Coming
through summons us to be faithful to the process of
reconciliation over time and space: coming through
hatred, coming through anger, coming through

alienation, coming through conflict, coming through war.

Being a midwife of reconciliation, no less than midwifing an actual birth, is bloody, and messy, and difficult. But it is also huge in significance, for being midwives to wounded humanity may just be our most important contribution to the healing of the world.

For Group Conversation and/or Journaling

The role of the midwife is to enter the lost places where new life is possible. What would you name as "lost places" in our world today?

What might be some everyday challenges that call you to midwife reconciliation and be a bearer of peace? How might you prepare to do this?

William Blake cites the capacity of Jesus to forgive another and reenter the deepest relation with another as the strongest evidence of Jesus' being God in the flesh. How do you react to this statement?

What activities (baking, walking, meditating, etc.) draw you into a contemplative space and a deepened relationship?

Breathprayer

Sit in silence for several minutes at the close of this time.

As you become aware of your breathing, pray this mantra or one of your own choosing as you breathe in and out:

Breathing in: In the heart of God

Breathing out: We are all found.

Closing Prayer:

Reconciling God,
your dream is of justice,
right relationship,
among all people.
Your heart is tender
towards the lost places in our lives.
Lead us to gentleness
with one another,
especially when our wounds
are most fresh.
May all that is lost
in us and in our world
come to be restored in your forgiving heart.
Amen. Let it be so.

MENTORING THE IMAGINATION

Bobbie, Golden Retriever
This sweet boy, made lovable by his quirky behavior, offered himself as a friend to all. Photographed in Middletown, New Jersey, and shared by my sister, Jean, whom he worshipped

Breathprayer

Sit in a comfortable position in silence. As you become aware of your breathing, pray this mantra or one of your own choosing as you breathe in and out.

Breathing in: Come, O God,

Breathing out: Dream in me.

For Reflection

Sometimes we have to imagine in order to see.

Bobbie was a Golden Retriever who lived with my sister's family in suburban New Jersey. Every morning, one of the family would open the back door and let him out into a spacious yard surrounded by a wire fence. After a few minutes, Bobbie would sit in front of the fence's small wire gate, waiting patiently for someone to open it so that he could go out and explore the neighborhood. This was his pattern for many years.

One day, my brother-in-law Kevin decided that the fence was no longer needed, so he spent the better part of a day removing the fence. By day's end, the fence had disappeared except for the small wire gate, a job saved for another time.

The next morning, Bobbie again stepped out into the back yard, only this time into a back yard almost entirely free of enclosure. In a space now nearly wide open on all sides, Bobbie went over to the remaining wire gate, sat in front of it, and waited. In spite of the family's beckoning him to the open space on all sides, Bobbie remained sitting in front of the little gate. Only when someone unlatched it did he venture out into the neighborhood. He clearly couldn't see that another way was possible.

This story speaks to what happens when the comfortable patterns of the past go unexamined, unchallenged, or unquestioned and stand in the way of imagining what might be new, life-giving possibilities. Truly, there are some things that have to be imagined in order to be seen, and a mentor's gift is to invite us into that deep seeing. We know this from the history of justice work, where we cherish and revisit the stories of giants who have helped move forward a more just, inclusive world order. At the same time, we also celebrate the prophetic individuals who mentored those giants in the ministry of imagination, who encouraged them to ask, "What does the world we want to live in look like?"

The first task is the act of imagination, observes the visionary Walter Brueggemann, who notes, "The prophet does not ask if the vision can be implemented, for questions of implementation are of no consequence until the vision can be imagined."[48] It is the vocation of the prophet to imagine, to be a harbinger of new ways of being and doing.

I suspect Brueggemann would encourage us to first give our energies over to asking, "What if?" "Why not?" and what Mary Oliver calls the big question, the one the world throws at us every morning, "Here you are, alive. Would you like to make a comment?"[49]

For every Oscar Romero,[50] who as a pious, conservative, quiet cleric initially sided with the landlords and ruthless death squads of El Salvador, there are countless Rutilio Grande's, refusing to write Romero off and instead reaching out to him, modeling another way to him, urging him to learn from the side of those who were poor and oppressed. Because of Grande's conviction and witness, Romero himself was able to embrace a new way of seeing and championing the rights of the most vulnerable. This is mentoring the imagination.

For every Joseph Cardinal Bernardin,[51] who in his early years as bishop emphasized to others the importance of prayer while, by his own admission, immersing himself in busyness and praying "on the run," there are dozens of faith-filled people calling out that a deep spiritual life rooted in justice cannot come to be without giving quality time to a relationship with God. This is mentoring the imagination.

Gaudium et Spes,[52] one of the documents of Vatican II, reminds us that the future of humanity is in the hands of those who are capable of providing others a hopeful vision of life, lifting up for others a future where God reigns in the hearts and lives of God's people. This is mentoring the imagination.

"What you are in love with, what seizes your imagination, will affect everything," declares Pedro Arrupe, SJ.[53] "It will decide what will get you out of bed in the morning, what you do with your evenings, how you spend your weekends, what you read, who you know, what breaks your heart, and what amazes you with joy and gratitude."

In our work for justice, let us celebrate the power of imagination and the gift of mentoring and being mentored into it. Mary Oliver might have been reflecting in this direction when she wrote about getting up in the morning and noticing a flock of crows. She remembers,

> *And now*
> *the crows break off from the rest of the darkness*
> *and burst up into the sky—as though*
> *all night they had thought of what they would like*
> *their lives to be, and imagined*
> *their strong, thick wings.*[54]

What would we like our lives and the lives of our neighbors to be, and can we imagine the wings to take us there?

Hopefully, as we live into that answer, we will both mentor and be mentored into just such imagining, so that our world—our precious, fragile, yearning world—can take flight towards God's dream that is whole and holy and imagined just so for each of us.

For Group Conversation and/or Journaling

Gaudium et Spes reminds us that the future of humanity is in the hands of those who can offer a hopeful vision of life. How do you keep hope alive?

Might there be any gates in your life that prevent you from seeing what is possible? Describe them.

What does the world you want to live in look like?

Breathprayer

Sit in silence for several minutes at the close of this time.

As you become aware of your breathing, pray this mantra or one of your own choosing as you breathe in and out.

Breathing in: Come, O God,

Breathing out: Dream in me.

Closing Prayer:

Dreaming God,
You are infinitely more
than we can ask or imagine.
Still, we try
to contain you and confine you,
to fit you within our human boundaries.
Help us break free
from a limited worldview.
Open our hearts.
Draw and direct our energies
to work for the abundant life you promise
for all of us.
Amen. Let it be so.

NOTES

These reflections are drawn from writing that spans nearly twenty years. I have endeavored to insure that sources and links are current and that these references will be helpful to the reader for any further reflection.

Staking Our Lives Against Dis-aster

[1]Madeleine L'Engle, *A Stone for a Pillow: Journeys with Jacob*. This definition is the substance of a reflection in *Sacred Journeys: A Woman's Book of Prayer* by Jan L. Richardson, "The Storied Life," (Nashville, Tennessee: Upper Room Books, 1995), 303.

[2]Ina Hughs, "A Prayer for Children," (New York: Fireside Books, 1995), xiv-xv. Much of the poet's writing was originally published in *The Knoxville News-Sentinel* and *The Charlotte Observer*.

[3]Marian Wright Edelman, Children's Defense Fund, effect of poverty on children in America.

[4]Marian Wright Edelman, Children's Defense Fund.

[5]USCCB, *Putting Children and Families First: A Challenge for Our Church, Nation, and World*, a statement of the United States Catholic Conference of Bishops, January 1, 1992.

[6]Marian Wright Edelman, Children's Defense Fund.

[7]Rainer Maria Rilke, *Ahead of All Parting: Selected Poetry and Prose*, translated by Stephen Mitchell, Modern Library Publishing.

Feeding the Lake

[8]Madeleine L'Engle, in *Walking on Water*, quoted
in *Spiritual Literacy: Reading the Sacred in Everyday
Life*, edited by Frederic and Mary Ann Brussat,
"Creativity" (New York: Scribner, 1996), 289.

[9]Madeleine L'Engle, in *A Circle of Quiet*, quoted
in *Sacred Journeys: A Woman's Book of Prayer* by Jan
L. Richardson, "The Storied Life," (Nashville,
Tennessee: Upper Room Books, 1995), 299.

[10]Madeleine L'Engle, in *A Circle of Quiet*, quoted
in *Sacred Journeys: A Woman's Book of Prayer*, "The
Storied Life," 299.

[11]Thich Nhat Hanh, in *Present Moment Wonderful
Moment*, quoted in *Spiritual Literacy: Reading the
Sacred in Everyday Life*, 522.

[12]Pax Christi USA, *Gathered in Peace: Forming Pax
Christi Communities*, Section 3, "Nonviolence,"
http://paxchristiusa1.files.wordpress.com/2011/01/g
athered-in-peace.pdf.

[13]Sheila Cassidy, in *Sharing the Darkness*, quoted
in *Spiritual Literacy: Reading the Sacred in Everyday
Life*, 355-356. The author writes of being
transformed by her experience as a doctor in Chile
and of her own arrest, imprisonment, and torture as
a prisoner of conscience.

[14]Thomas Merton, "Letter to a Young
Activist," *Essential Writings*, selected and with an
introduction by Christine M. Bochen (Maryknoll,
New York: Orbis Books, 2000).

[15] Joanna Macy, "Working through Environmental Despair,"*Ecopsychology*, Roszak, Gomes, and Kanner, editors (Sierra Club, 1995).

Sending the Great Blue Heron

[16]Frederic and Mary Ann Brussat, *Spiritual Literacy: Reading the Sacred in Everyday Life*, "Places," (New York: Scribner, 1996), 101.

[17]Jesuit Refugee Services, www.jrsusa.org. The mission of Jesuit Refugee Services is to accompany, serve and advocate for the rights of refugees and forcibly displaced people.

[18]Frederic and Mary Ann Brussat, *Spiritual Literacy: Reading the Sacred in Everyday Life*, "Practicing Spiritual Literacy: Places," *118-119*.

Tracing Our Journeys

[19]Wendy Wright, in *Sacred Heart: A Gateway to God*, quoted in *A Maryknoll Book of Inspiration, Readings for Every Day of the Year*, edited by Michael Leach and Doris Goodnough (Maryknoll, New York: Orbis Books, 2010), 291-292.

[20]*Hope and Solidarity: Jon Sobrino's Challenge to Christian Theology*, edited by Stephen J. Pope (Maryknoll, New York: Orbis Books, 2008)

[21]Marie Dennis, Cynthia Moe-Lobeda, Joseph Nangle, OFM, Stuart Taylor, *St. Francis and the Foolishness of God* (Maryknoll, New York: Orbis Books, 1993).

Making Mystical Space

[22]Robert Sardello, *Facing the World with Soul: The Reimagination of Modern Life* (Great Barrington, Massachusetts: Lindisfarne Press, 1991, 2004), quoted in *Spiritual Literacy, Reading the Sacred in Everyday Life,* edited by Frederic and Mary Ann Brussat, "Places" (New York: Scribner, 1996), 112-113.

Becoming a "We"

[23]Barbara Brown Taylor, *An Altar in the World: A Geography of Faith,* "The Practice of Carrying Water," (New York: HarperCollins, 2009), 153.
[24]Marilou Awiakta, "When Earth Becomes an It," *Selu: Seeking the Corn-Mother's Wisdom* (Golden, Colorado: Fulcrum, 1993).
[25]Wesley Granberg-Michaelson, "Renewing the Whole Creation," *Holy Ground: A Resource on Faith and the Environment* (edited by Sojourners, 2000).
[26]George Tinker, "For All My Relations," *Holy Ground: A Resource on Faith and the Environment* (edited by Sojourners, 2000). Also referenced at http://seasonofcreation.com/wp-content/uploads/2010/04/a-theology-of-kinship-with-creation.pdf

Taking It Personally

[27]Julia Esquivel, "The Sigh," *The Certainty of Spring: Poems by a Guatemalan Exile,* with Anne Woehrle, 1992.

[28]Elizabeth O'Connor, *The New Community,* 1976.

[29]Maryknoll Mission Society, Priests, Brothers, Sisters, Lay Volunteers, 55 Ryder Road, Ossining, New York 10562.

Casting a Wider Net

[30]Dr. Martin Luther King, Jr., "Letter from a Birmingham Jail," April 16, 1963. Dr. King had gone to Birmingham to participate in a march already taking place to desegregate the downtown shopping area.

Embodying Justice

[31]Robert J. Wicks, *Everyday Simplicity: A Practical Guide to Spiritual Growth,* "Faithfulness" (Notre Dame, Indiana: Sorin Books, 2000), 34.

[32]Rabbi Greg Harris, *Tikkun Olam: Moving Us Beyond Ourselves,* http://www.bethelmc.org/LinkClick.aspx ?fileticket=0cuJSxP2UYI%3D&tabid=367. Harris describes the march in Selma where Rabbi Heschel joined Dr. King in a visible reminder that Jewish

piety dictates action (praying with our feet), in
addition to ritual piety.

[33]"Patient Endurance,"
http://blog.greenhearted.org/2011/11/patient-
endurance.html

[34]Barbara Kingsolver, *Animal Dreams* (New York:
HarperCollins Publisher, 1990).

[35]Thomas Cullinan, OSB, *Peacemaking: Day by Day,*
referenced in "Patient Endurance,"
http://blog.greenhearted.org/2011/11/patient-
endurance.html

[36]Jacques Lusseyran, *And There Was Light* (Sandpoint,
Idaho: Little, Brown, and Company, 1963). This
autobiography of the blind French resistance fighter
is also referenced in the blog,
http://peacefulbodyschool.com/tag/jacques-
lusseyran/

Living on the Bridge

[37]Jesuit Refugee Service/USA,
http://jrsusa.org/accompaniment, "Our
accompaniment affirms that God is present in
human history, even in its most tragic episodes."

[38]Dr. Christina Pourgourides, a psychiatrist working
tirelessly on behalf of refugees in the United
Kingdom and named by the World Health
Association as one of the world's most caring
physicians. http://news.bbc.co.uk/2/hi/health/44500
02.stm

[39]Alby Stone, "The Perilous Bridge," an explanation of the significance of bridges in the Celtic world, http://www.indigogroup.co.uk/edge/pbridge.htm

Working from Our Hearts into Our Hands

[40]These words are widely attributed to the Buddha, although some dispute their authenticity. The quote sometimes reads, "Your work is to discover your work and then, with all your heart, give yourself to it."

[41]"The Church in the Modern World," "Gaudium et spes," 43. *Vatican Council II, the Conciliar and Post-Conciliar Documents, New Revised Edition,* edited by Austin Flannery, OP (Northport, New York: Costello Publishing Company, Fourth Printing, 1998).

[42]United States Conference of Catholic Bishops (USCCB), *Everyday Christianity: to Hunger and Thirst for Justice,* a Pastoral Reflection on Lay Discipleship for Justice in a New Millennium, 1998.

[43]Brenda Peterson, *Nature and Other Mothers: Reflections on the Feminine in Everyday Life* (Ballantine Books, 1992).

[44]Norvene Vest, *A Benedictine Spirituality of Work.* Currently out of print.

[45]Brian Andreas, *Story People,* "Imagining World," www.storypeople.com

Midwifing Reconciliation

[46]Christin Lore Weber, *A Womanchrist Reflection on the Beatitudes* (HarperCollins, 1st edition, 1989).
[47]Douglas V. Steere, *Dimensions of Prayer* (Nashville, Tennessee: Upper Room Books). This is a revised edition of this Quaker scholar's 1962 *Dimensions of Prayer*.

Mentoring the Imagination

[48]Walter Brueggemann, *The Prophetic Imagination* (Minneapolis, Minnesota: Augsburg Fortress, 2nd edition), 2010.
[49]Mary Oliver, in the foreword of *Long Life: Essays and Other Writing*
[50]Renny Golden, "Oscar Romero: Bishop of the Poor" (*U.S.Catholic*, published on USCatholic.org, www.uscatholic.org/culture/social-justice/2009/02/oscar-romero-bishop-poor. When Romero attended the funeral of Rutilio Grande, he was faced with the peasants' unspoken question, "Will you stand with us as Rutilio did?" This was a turning point in his life.
[51]Joseph Cardinal Bernardin, *The Gift of Peace,* "Letting Go"(New York: Image Books, Doubleday, 1997), 3-11.
[52]"The Church in the Modern World," "Gaudium et spes," 4. *Vatican Council II, the Conciliar and Post-Conciliar Documents, New Revised Edition,* edited by Austin Flannery, OP (Northport, New York:

Costello Publishing Company, Fourth Printing, 1998).

[53]Father Pedro Arrupe, SJ, "Fall in Love," in *Finding God in All Things: A Marquette Prayer Book* (Marquette University Press, 2009).

[54]Mary Oliver, "Landscape," *New and Selected Poems* (Boston: Beacon Press, 1992), 129.

~~~

Printed by CreateSpace, an Amazon.com Company